WORLD'S STRANGEST ANIMAL FACTS

Jocelyn Little

Illustrated by Neecy Twinem

 Sterling Publishing Co., Inc. New York

Edited by Claire Bazinet

Library of Congress Cataloging-in-Publication Data

Little, Jocelyn.
    World's strangest animal facts / Jocelyn Little ; illustrated by Neecy Twinem.
        p.   cm.
    Includes index.
    ISBN 0-8069-8520-8
    1. Animals—Miscellanea—Juvenile literature. [1. Animals—Miscellanea. 2.
Curiosities and wonders.] I. Twinem, Neecy, ill. II. Title.
    QL49.L76   1994
    591—dc20   93-47248
                                                  CIP
                                                  AC

10 9 8 7 6 5 4 3 2

First paperback edition published in 1995 by
Sterling Publishing Company, Inc.
387 Park Avenue South, New York, N.Y. 10016
© 1994 by Jocelyn Little
Illustrations © 1994 by Neecy Twinem
Distributed in Canada by Sterling Publishing
% Canadian Manda Group, One Atlantic Avenue, Suite 105
Toronto, Ontario, Canada M6K 3E7
Distributed in Great Britain and Europe by Cassell PLC
Villiers House, 41/47 Strand, London WC2N 5JE, England
Distributed in Australia by Capricorn Link (Australia) Pty Ltd.
P.O. Box 6651, Baulkham Hills, Business Centre, NSW 2153, Australia
Manufactured in the United States of America
All rights reserved

Sterling ISBN 0-8069-8520-8 Trade
              0-8069-8521-6 Paper

To the loving memory
of my mother, Alice Little,
and my friend Alan Preston

Foreword

This book would not exist without the contributions of my sister, Janet Little. It began as a conversation between us, and though this end product only faintly resembles the original, its basic framework remains. Janet wrote the chapter titles, and the facts were gathered and organized around them. She also did the thankless job of deciding which should go first, and which after. I am indebted to her untiring support and good humor, which made writing this a joy. Although her name does not appear on the cover, the contents have been greatly improved by her contributions.

Contents

Ancient Animals

Crocodiles are not only older than us humans, they are older than dinosaurs, older than flowers, older than the continent of Africa.

Giant crocodiles forty-five to sixty feet long roamed the Big Bend area of West Texas. Their teeth were six inches long.

Whales once roamed the land. Modern whales evolved from a creature with legs; and they still have a vestigial hipbone. These land creatures in turn evolved from sea dwellers, and returned to the sea about seventy million years ago.

There were once elephants that were only the size of pigs. They lived in the islands of the Mediterranean. There were also dwarf mammoths in North America, which grew to about the size of a modern cow.

House cats evolved from desert creatures that were adapted to deal with hot dry air. It is thought that is why cats don't like to get wet.

Cassowaries are big flightless birds, like ostriches. They are born without even vestigial wing bones. It is thought that they are direct

7

descendants of two-legged, warm-blooded, non-reptilian dinosaurs, and that nowhere along their history did these birds fly.

Penguins once stood five feet tall and weighed about three hundred pounds. Some scientists have observed that they would have made fine football players. The emperor penguin, currently the largest, stands four feet tall and weighs a hundred pounds.

Ever since dodos became extinct in 1681, no new *calvaria* trees have grown in the island of Mauritius. An American ecologist, Dr. Temple, theorized that the seeds of the *calvaria* needed to pass through the gizzard of the dodo in order to germinate. In 1973, there were only thirteen trees left, so Dr. Temple fed their seeds to turkeys and then planted them. Three *calvaria* trees sprouted, the first new ones in three hundred years.

The largest animal ever to have flown, *Quetzacoatalus*, lived in Texas one hundred and fifty to two hundred million years ago. Conservative estimates give their wingspan as between thirty-three and fifty feet across. (An average small airplane has a wingspan of twenty-five feet.) These animals were like huge vultures, feeding on the decaying flesh of dinosaurs.

Pterosaurs, the first flyers, were neither reptiles nor birds. They were warm-blooded, and examinations of their cranial cavities reveal that they were probably more intelligent than any reptile living today. A fossil found in Russia in 1970, preserved in extraordinary detail, had impressions of a thick coat of body fur which extended over the wings.

Ernest Wood of Eastland, Texas, put "Old Rip," a horned toad, in the cornerstone of a court house in 1897. He took it out, alive, thirty-one years later, on February 17, 1928. Old Rip lived another two years, until January 1930, when he perished of pneumonia.

Chinese villagers in Chouaoutien, near Peking, were familiar with a limestone hill rich in fossil bone when Western archaeologists arrived in 1903. In fact, a pharmacist had been grinding up the fossil bones to use as medicines for generations. What the Chinese did not know was that some of the bones were those of their human ancestors—half a million years old.

Only twenty thousand years ago, one-third of the world was covered in mile-thick ice. Our Cro-Magnon ancestors speared mastodons in Spain and reindeer in France. In the New World, walruses lay on the beaches of South Carolina and mastodons and musk-oxen roamed New York State.

Beavers were once the size of bears. A kind of bison had horns eight feet wide and condors flew on twelve-foot wings. This was about a hundred thousand years ago.

Prehistoric hogs stood five feet at the shoulder and roamed the American Midwest.

Three million years ago, in what is now Australia, there lived a kind of kangaroo that was over nine feet tall. There was also a wombat the size of a rhinoceros and a giant koala.

Spiders were once nine feet long. They were sea scorpions, the size of lions or gorillas, and they ranged the earth in the Silurian era, a time of warm, quiet seas. Their fossils are among the most ancient records of animal life on earth.

There was once a lion which had a pouch like a kangaroo. This lion was the size of a large dog and was a highly specialized plant-eater.

An extinct form of rhinoceros in Mongolia was taller than a giraffe. Specimens were found of rhinos twenty-five feet tall, compared to the living giraffe's eighteen feet.

Centipedes were twenty-five feet long in prehistoric times. Dragonflies once had wingspans of nearly three feet. They were the biggest bugs ever.

A brontosaurus' tongue weighed four tons, the same size as a whole adult African elephant today.

The dinosaur *Tricerotops* weighed one and three-quarter tons, was twenty-five feet long, and had a brain the size of a walnut. Another dinosaur had a separate brain in its tail to move its big behind.

Most dinosaurs were the size of chickens.

Nesting and Resting

If you inject a rabbit with the blood of a sleeping rabbit, it goes to sleep.

Many birds sleep on the wing. Birds which have to fly over enormous expanses of ocean, especially, sleep as they fly. Some birds have been clocked as flying for from sixty to ninety hours at a stretch.

Swifts sometimes take naps by gripping the wings of flying airplanes with their feet.

Baby chicks, while still in their eggs, dream. Newborn kittens dream before their eyes ever open.

Families of sea otters entangle themselves in beds of seaweed at twilight, binding themselves into a raft which holds them secure and together till dawn.

Seals sleep only one and a half minutes at a time.

Hibernating woodchucks breathe ten times an hour. Active wood-chucks breathe twenty-one hundred times an hour.

The dormouse is one of the legendary "seven sleepers," or hibernators, of the animal world; the others being the badger, bat, bear, marmot, hedgehog, and ground squirrel. A curled-up hibernating dormouse can be rolled across a table or tossed in the air and it won't wake up. The garden dormouse will eat any other that begins its winter sleep before it does, even its own mother.

The West African lungfish has to come up to the surface to breathe from time to time. When the swamps dry out, lungfish dig a burrow and surround themselves with a cocoon of mucus, in which they can live for up to four years, until the rains come again.

The jewel beetle has one of the longest life spans in the insect world. They feed exclusively on wood, and the eggs are laid under the bark of a live tree. The larvae bore into the tree, continuing even if the tree is cut and made into furniture, for as long as forty years, until the adult finally emerges.

Mayflies live for only six hours, but their eggs take four years before the adults are ready to emerge.

The largest moth, the Hercules, has a fourteen-inch wingspan. It lives for fourteen days and eats nothing.

Monarch butterflies, migrating to Mexico, are increasingly using offshore oil-rig platforms to rest overnight. Workers in the Gulf of Mexico report enjoying the spectacle of thousands of the orange-and-black butterflies clinging to the metal rigging at sunset and then departing at dawn.

The fairy tern lays eggs in the forks of trees without building a nest at all. Fortunately, the young are born and grow up quickly.

Harvester ants in western Colorado use fossil shark teeth in the construction of their mounds. They also use broken glass and particles of green jade as shingles.

The record for a beaver dam goes to an industrious pair in Berlin, New Hampshire, who built one four thousand feet long.

The bizcacha is a curious rodent that lives on the pampas of Argentina. "In the evenings the bizcachas come out in numbers, and quietly sit at the mouths of their burrows on their haunches," wrote Charles Darwin. "At such times they are very tame, and a man on horseback passing by seems only to present an object for their grave contemplation." A strange habit of the rodent was to drag every solid object available into a pile near his burrow entrance. A man who lost his watch or his pipe had only to search these piles to find it. Cattle bones, thistle stalks, stones, hard lumps of earth or dung, and other objects formed these collections. Darwin could not explain their use.

Badgers air their bedding in the spring.

Hippos give birth and nurse underwater.

A warm winter in the Arctic can be fatal to harp seals. Females need to crawl out on the ice to give birth. If there is no ice, the pups drown.

Newborn giraffes come to life with a jolt, falling six feet to the ground. A baby giraffe born at Whipsnade Zoo near London measured five feet two inches. A day later it was six feet three inches tall. This means it was growing at a rate of one-half inch per *hour*.

The paradoxical frog is between seven and ten inches in length as a tadpole. When they reach adulthood, however, these frogs *shrink* to a mere two inches or less in length.

A newborn crocodile is three times as large as the egg it came out of.

An Australian frog named **Rheobatrachus silus**, which unfortunately recently became extinct, incubated its young inside the female's stomach. The eggs became tadpoles and the tadpoles froglets before they were finally vomited forth into the world.

The hydroid, a marine animal, produces jellyfish as offspring. The jellyfish, in turn, have little hydroids, like their grandparents.

The female red flying frog of Sumatra, a great jumper, can sense puddles no bigger than a dinner plate ten to twelve feet below her in the dark of the jungle night. When ready to lay her eggs, she climbs through the limbs of trees until she senses a protected pool far below her. She is so positive of her find that she lays a mass of foamy eggs on the branch. Within a few days, the eggs hatch and the tadpoles fall from the tree to land in the pool, their first taste of flying. When grown, the frogs use their feet as parachutes and sail down from trees.

The female of the blind salamander called *Proteus anguinus*, found in caves in Yugoslavia, has the option of laying eggs or retaining them in her body and bearing live young.

Reptile eggs hatch out into males or females depending on how warmly they are incubated. Warm nests produce baby male turtles, crocodiles, snakes, and the like, while cooler nests produce baby females.

There is no such thing as a male Amazon molly. All of these fish are female, and they lay eggs which carry all of the information needed to make new fish. Sperm from another kind of fish, such as the sailfish molly, stimulates the eggs to grow but does not contribute to the new life.

The whelk lays up to two thousand eggs at a time, but only ten to thirty whelk survive. The others devour each other.

Every hamster in the world is descended from a single female who was found in Syria in 1930 with twelve babies.

An opossum mother can have up to fifteen little ones at a time. The entire litter can fit in a teaspoon.

About thirty years ago, a thatched roof in Denmark caught fire. Living on that roof was a stork and her young. The mother bird refused to abandon her babies to the flames, instead sheltering them beneath her wings, which she beat wildly to drive off the choking smoke. When the fire was put out, the stork was black with soot, but all survived.

Emperor penguins have such heightened maternal instincts that they will pick up stones, dead chicks, frozen or ruined eggs, and try to incubate them. The adults compete to raise orphaned young.

When a male flightless cormorant of the Galapagos Islands comes to relieve his mate of egg-sitting duty, he invariably presents her with a tasty starfish or a "bouquet" of lovely seaweed.

Hoatzins are bizarre birds that live in South American swamps. The babies are born with claws on their wings to help them clamber around the trees. The babies can also swim and dive, climbing back up into their nest tree when the predator leaves. Hoatzins primarily eat green leaves, which they digest as cows do. In fact, they even smell like cows—cow dung, to be precise.

The young of the yellow-billed cuckoo of North America are born with a black leathery skin that makes them look more like baby porcupines than baby birds. When the day arrives to learn to fly, the skin sheath bursts and the birds' feathers appear, ready for use.

European cuckoos lay eggs in other birds' nests for incubating. Each female cuckoo chooses a species to parasitize and is able to lay eggs that match the host eggs in color and markings to an astonishing degree.

The murre, a kind of seabird, has unusual eggs. When fried, the "white" is blue and the yolk is blood-red.

Cassowary eggs have uncolored outer shells and are green inside.

Chilean tinamous lay black eggs. On occasion, though, the eggs turn out primrose, sage-green, light indigo, chocolate-brown, or pinkish orange.

Emus have dark green eggs.

Even chickens lay multi-colored eggs if bred to do so. Chilean strains produce blue, green, pink, and olive eggs.

Beastly Behavior

Wild chimpanzees often bow and shake hands to say hello. All apes, monkeys, and almost all lemurs smile. Chimpanzees, orangutans, and gorillas all laugh heartily. Baby otters and fawns play hide-and-seek, and young chimps play peek-a-boo, giggling with joy.

Chimpanzees in the London Zoo were observed pantomiming people eating. They mimed an entire tea party, sitting at a table, pouring, eating, and passing utensils and food, with nothing but their imaginations providing the supplies.

Deep in the jungles of the Congo are great flattened and much-trodden swampy areas where the pygmies say the elephants used to dance.

A frightened elephant will stick its ears straight up.

Elephants have funerals. An elephant in the Sudan was killed and the hunter returned the next day to find the elephant's body had been buried in eighteen inches of soil. According to all the signs, other elephants had dug the grave with their tusks.

Dr. Robert Cushman Murphy of the American Museum of Natural History found a penguin graveyard on South Georgia Island near the Antarctic. In a small clear lake some distance from the ocean were the bodies of thousands of penguins, preserved by the cold. Around the edges of the lake were sick and injured birds. This is the only case of a common burial ground in animals other than man to be discovered and substantiated.

Societies of birds have been observed to hold "trials" culminating in the death of the accused. Crows and rooks have been seen to surround a member of their own species, cawing loudly, and then pecking it to death. Storks in Berlin and flamingos in Bengal have likewise been observed executing one of their own. A Father Bougeant watched as martins sealed up the small opening of one of their nests, walling up alive the sparrow that had stolen it.

Towards the end of the 1800s, herds of springboks, a kind of gazelle, fifty thousand strong, roamed the plains of South Africa. There are reports that the springboks would surround an inexperienced lion and force him to march along until he starved or was trampled.

Mother koalas spank their babies on their bottoms.

Gorillas never physically chastise their young.

A Dutch scientist tied a chick to a tree on a jungle path, then watched as a troop of chimpanzees gently freed the baby bird.

When a chimpanzee gets angry, it is more likely to vent its rage on a tree than to take it out on a member of its troop.

The chatter of chimpanzees that preceded a thunderstorm was recorded one day in 1962 at the Bronx Zoo in New York. Later, on a sunny day, the tape was played back. The chimps stopped in confusion, and then dashed for shelter.

Professor Konrad Lorenz, who with Niko Tinbergen founded the scientific study of animal behavior, eventually mastered the language of geese to such an extent that he could direct their movements. Here are some of his interpretations:

"ga ga ga ga ga ga ga": It's nice here. There's lots of food. Let's stay.

"ga ga ga ga ga ga": This grass is no good. Let's move along soon.

"ga ga ga ga ga": Move a little faster.

"ga ga ga ga": Faster! Stretch your neck out.

"ga ga ga": Waddle as fast as you can. We're on alert. Prepare for takeoff.

"ga gi ga": Waddle fast but don't fly.

a single nasal "ra": Take off immediately, everyone!

a low continuous cackle: All clear.

Professor Hubert Frings of the University of Pennsylvania studied the language of crows. He found that there are distinct dialects which are unintelligible to other "provincial" crows. Some more "cosmopolitan" crows have mastered other dialects as well as important jackdaw and gull calls. "Provincial" crows have to attend an "international crow language school" for at least a year to learn other languages. There are at least three hundred distinct calls.

A dictionary of squirrel language was published by Jan C. Taylor of the Ministry of Agriculture in Surrey, England, in 1966.

There are bees that gang together, attack and pummel worker bees, and steal their nectar. Bee police are said to be outnumbered.

Marguerite Combes watched an ant fire brigade in action. Combes, a scientist at Fontainebleau in 1930, dropped a lighted match near an ant colony. The ants advanced in a body and deliberately squirted formic acid at the flame. She watched them press down on their stomachs to make the most of their jets. When the flame was extinguished, they went back to their little ant duties.

Some ants stretch and yawn when they wake up.

The bulldog ant bathes daily. Their poison is like a venom of a bee, and the bite of one can be deadly.

There's a kind of ant that bakes its own bread. Called the Dalmatie, it chews up grain, makes it into patties, and leaves it to bake in the sun.

Ants keep herds of aphids in corrals and milk them daily. Ants which live on coffee plantations in Surinam have an unusual method of ensuring a food supply. At swarming time, the winged females choose aphids that are young and already mated. They pick them up and carry them on their nuptial flight, holding them in their jaws while mating. When the ants return to earth, these living dowries are deposited on coffee roots, where they begin to produce sugar for the new colony.

A farmer in Washington tried everything to get rid of the crows that were ravaging his crops. Finally, he soaked almonds in strychnine and put them out. Two crows ate them and dropped dead. Within minutes the remaining crows made a low sad cry, apparently a message of death, and the flock in their thousands took wing, never to return.

Worker termite messages are coded in their saliva, which they spit into the mouth of their queen. If a worker termite is encased in a steel box far from its queen, it will respond to an unseen, unheard, unsmelled influence that tells it to go home. It will try to pierce the unpierceable walls, always in the direction of the queen. If she is killed, the worker termite subsides into apathy.

Bees create their own air conditioning. When it gets really hot and the wax of the hive threatens to melt, they bring in water and pour it in a fine film over the combs. Then a group of bees station themselves at the entrance to the colony while another group stays inside. Both groups flap their wings as fast as four hundred times a second. In this way, they create a cross-draft which pulls the hot air out and the cool air into the hive.

The blood fluke is a terrible parasite which afflicts more than a hundred million people yearly. During its complicated life cycle it must pass from a snail host to sheep or cattle. The infected snails expel mucus, which is then eaten by ants. A single parasite makes its way to the ant's brain, takes over the nerve center, and henceforth guides the ant's behavior. Like little robots, the ants are compelled to climb to the tips of grass blades and cling there for hours, stuffed with parasites. In the words of William Hohorst, German parasitologist, they "literally offer themselves to be eaten" by sheep and cattle.

Some butterflies live longer without their heads than with them. If the heads of caterpillars are removed with a minimum loss of blood, the caterpillars will continue their normal development, become chrysalises, and emerge as healthy, headless butterflies. Scientists have concluded that the headless butterflies lead a more placid life than their whole counterparts and therefore live longer.

Some animals are born with two heads, both of which function. Dudley-Duplex, a two-headed king snake of the San Diego Zoo, was one such beast. One night one head got hungry and tried to eat the other. Zookeepers separated the two, but the following night the two heads fought again, and this time the snake killed itself.

On October 18, 1987, the Associated Press reported a school of dolphins surrounded a small boat and pushed it in the direction of a buoy. There the man in the boat found a young dolphin entangled in the anchor rope. He freed the animal and the other dolphins began whistling with joy, leaping out of the water and following the boat until it reached port.

Notions of Motion

Spiderlings go ballooning in the spring and autumn. Right after hatching they run swiftly up stems to the tips of plants, and spin out silk so they can be carried away by the wind. They adjust their threads like sailors, maneuvring around trees and houses. Spiderlings rise as high as 14,000 feet, and may stay aloft for weeks. The word "gossamer" comes from "goose summer," the season when the delicate spider parachutes fall to earth, looking like silvery feathers in the trees and fields.

Arctic terns fly from the Antarctic to the Arctic and back, spending ten months of the year in the air. The little ones make the ten-thousand-mile trip on their own, arriving at an exact place they've never been to before, and the adults follow.

Hummingbirds hitch rides north tucked in the feathers of migrating Canada geese.

The black-necked swan carries its young on its back like a true

Mother Goose. The jacana is a bird which flies with its babies tucked under its wings, their large toes dangling.

The Abyssinian blue goose can fly backwards.

Tropical jumping vipers, African carpet vipers, and East Asian tree snakes spring through the air like real live jack-in-the-boxes. They coil like a spring and then straighten explosively. Tree snakes can also flatten their rib cages and glide gracefully from branch to branch and from tree to ground like paper airplanes.

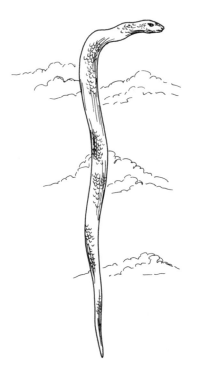

Snakes have been seen using vertical leaps as a way of travelling down hillsides. A Mary Lupton wrote that, in 1926, she and her husband were walking up a remote mountain in Italy when a five-foot-long snake leaped, rigid and vertical, over their heads, landed coiled behind them, and continued to launch itself downhill, looking like a long stick being thrown up into the air.

The springtail, a kind of insect, hops on a pogo-stick-like appendage on its underside. It can leap many hundreds of times the height of its body.

Professor Otto Koehler of Freiburg University was riding a bicycle in the country when he hit a hole and the rear wheel buckled. As he was a long way from help, he went on, despite an uncomfortable bouncing motion. He was soon joined by a young rabbit, who followed despite all of Koehler's attempts to shoo it away. Prof. Koehler came to the conclusion that young rabbits will follow anything that hops.

Professor Niko Tinbergen, the cofounder of the science of ethology, was riding a bicycle through a wood. A young fawn followed him. The fawn had seen the white mudguard on Tinbergen's bicycle and followed it as it would have followed its mother's white tail.

Flying squids travel in large schools and often leap eighteen feet in the air, landing on the decks of ships.

A large school of fish was being threatened by a barracuda in the Indian Ocean. Instantly, the school assumed a formation that looked like a giant shark and leaped high in the air, like a dolphin, four times in quick succession. The barracuda paused in astonishment, then fled in terror.

Elephant-trunk fish navigate in the murky waters of the Nile by surrounding themselves with an electric field.

Hydras live underwater and move by turning cartwheels on their tentacles. They look like disembodied hands.

The great French entomologist Jean Henri Fabre once sent a line of processionary caterpillars walking around the rim of a vase in an unbroken circle. These caterpillars follow each other blindly, head to tail. Fabre's caterpillars marched around and around for a solid week, only finding their way back to their nest on the eighth day.

Sometimes a flock of sheep develop the bad habit of leaping fences and wandering off. To cure this, the shepherd merely has to tie back the ears of the lead ram. Sheep always point their ears forward when they jump, and if you tie their ears back, they can't jump.

Bored Royal Air Force pilots stationed in the Falkland Islands have come up with what they call "a marvelous new game." They look for a beach crowded with penguins and fly slowly along at the water's edge. Ten thousand penguins turn their heads in perfect unison watching the plane fly by, and when the plane circles and comes back, they watch like mass spectators at a slow-motion tennis match. Then the pilot flies out to sea and straight back over the penguin colony, and heads look up, up, up, and ten thousand penguins fall flat on their backs.

Clever Creatures

In 1966, pigeons were used in factories to inspect gelatin capsules, removing the defective ones. They proved to be exemplary workers, but the project was scrapped when it seemed that the public was dubious about consuming drugs inspected by pigeons.

Shortly afterwards, pigeons were also used in factory inspection lines to check diodes. They performed at a rate of one thousand inspections an hour (their rate was entirely voluntary) and had a ninety-eight-percent success rate, which seemed to improve the longer they worked. However, they too were laid off due to the low opinion the public held of their abilities.

Pigeons have been trained by the U.S. Coast Guard Service to spot people lost at sea, provided they are wearing their yellow life jackets. So wear your life jacket at sea! There might be a pigeon looking for you.

Pigeons at Harvard were taught to look at color slides and indicate whether there were any humans in the frame. The birds quickly became better at it than their human teachers, according to Professor Robert Herrnstein, who also taught the pigeons to indicate if the photos included trees, bodies of water, or other objects.

Many parrots can talk, but Alex, the African grey, knows what the words mean. He lives with Irene Pepperberg, and when the bird got sick a few years ago, she had to leave him at the vet's office overnight. As she was leaving, Alex called out: "Come here. I love you. I'm sorry. Wanna go back."

Colonel P. H. Fawcett, a well-known nineteenth-century South American explorer, who eventually vanished into the Amazon jungle, reported that birds in the Andean mountains rubbed hard rock with the leaves of a small red plant. The stone then became soft enough for the birds to peck holes in it. Fawcett theorized that this was the method used by ancient Incan masons to fit huge stones together so tightly a razor cannot be inserted between them, forming walls strong enough to withstand earthquakes after many centuries. The plant has never been found.

Professor Otto Koehler of the University of Freiburg, in reports published between 1940 and 1953, demonstrated that pigeons can count to five. Parrots and jackdaws can count to six, and ravens, Amazon parrots, grey parrots, and squirrels can count to the number seven.

Elizabeth Mann Borgese also found reports that in Thailand some banks employ monkeys. They are more reliable than humans in detecting counterfeit money. "Bank apes," trained for at least two years, are worth $5,000. She also states that three neatly dressed chimps work in a furniture factory in Houston.

A pair of chimpanzees tend bar in Amsterdam, pouring drinks, carrying orders to tables, and lighting cigarettes. Otto and Jimmy became Dutch TV stars and Otto learned to drive a car. Once Otto was allowed to take the controls of his owner's private plane!

Jimmy has developed the habit of kissing ladies and also lifting their skirts, something his owner did *not* teach him.

In the Munich Zoo, a chimpanzee watched the attendant unlock his cage with a key. The chimp made himself a key by chewing the end of a stick until it fit the lock, unlocked his cage, and escaped.

Koko is a gorilla who has been taught sign language. She jokes, curses, insults her teachers, teaches other gorillas sign language, makes up words for unfamiliar objects, and sometimes lies. She understands and responds to spoken and written English as readily as to signs. When asked how gorillas talk, she beats her chest. When asked to point to a scary picture in a magazine, Koko pushed a mirror into the face of her instructor. In response to the question "Where do gorillas go when they die?" she said, "Comfortable hole bye." When Koko first met other gorillas, she called them "dirty alligators."

Washoe, the famous chimp who was the first to be taught sign language, was raised in the exclusive company of humans. When she was first introduced to other chimpanzees, she labelled them "black bugs."

Both elephants and chimpanzees have been trained to paint abstract pictures, the finer examples of which sell for high prices. And a dog, Arli, wrote poetry, which a well-known critic described as "charming" and as having "a definite affinity with the 'concretist' groups."

Arli wrote on a specially adapted typewriter. One day his trainer, Elizabeth Borgese, was dictating to him, but he had other ideas. Curious, she let him go ahead. Arli typed "A BAD A BAD

DOOG." Another day, when asked where he wanted to go, the dog typed "CAR."

Jim the Wonder Dog was a Llewellyn setter who was studied by experts from the School of Education at the University of Missouri in 1933. He could identify trees, pick out a license plate when asked in French, and identify individuals in a crowd in German. Jim predicted the winning horses of six consecutive Kentucky Derby races, and that Roosevelt would win the 1936 election when most people said he would lose.

A Chinese newspaper reported that dogs which could receive commands in Dutch, English, German, Malay, and Chinese had been awarded degrees from the University of Malay. The article also mentioned that Professor Uncoo Asiz was outraged over this, stating that their standards were far too high for dogs.

CNN News, on July 12, 1990, reported that a stray dog named Blackie in Sri Lanka had been taught to add, subtract, divide, and multiply. His owner was training him for the circus when he noticed his unusual ability.

A trained dog of Mannheim, Germany, was found to have a mathematical ability superior to that of an average adult human being. This dog could count the flowers in a vase after seeing them for only a second, while humans had to remove the flowers in order to count them individually.

When he was shown the famous optical illusion:

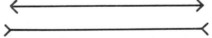

and asked which line was longer, the dog answered correctly, "both equal," while human observers got it wrong.

Chris was a psychic mutt who lived in Greenwich, Rhode Island, in the 1950s. After he foretold the winning horses at a daily double, parapsychologists from Duke University tested him extensively and concluded he was clairvoyant. He was only a day off in predicting his own death.

Lady Wonder was a famous psychic horse who lived from 1926 to 1957 and communicated on a large typewriter like Arli's. She predicted Truman's re-election, that the United States would enter World War II, and in 1951 made headlines by directing police to the site of the body of a boy who had been missing for two years.

Karl Krall of Elberfeld, Germany, had a stable of very smart horses in the late 1800s. They could read, tell time, and identify pictures of people. Berto the blind stallion was good at arithmetic. The horse Muhamed, with a sack tied over his head, could do cube roots. Krall once asked one of the horses why he didn't talk like people do. After painful efforts with his mouth, the horse spelled out in a number alphabet: "Because I haven't got a good voice."

It is believed that horses may see us as bigger than we really are, which makes them easy to tame. When approaching a strange horse, do so from the front, with your arms at your sides. Lean forward and blow through your nostrils, as this is what horses do when saying hello.

The horse trainer Henry Blake put together a "dictionary of horse language" in his fascinating book, *Talking with Horses*. Some of the messages which are communicated by gesture and voice are:

> I am only small.
> Let us get the hell out of here.
> Mummy loves you.
> Oh my God!
> That tickles.
> We are good girls here.
> Where is my bloody breakfast?

Godolphin Arabian was one of only three horses from which all modern thoroughbreds are descended. He was being used as a cart horse when his potential was discovered. He lived a long life, but died after accidentally killing the cat that shared his stable: he refused to eat or drink after kicking his small friend to death.

Fred Walker spent some time on a farm in California, plowing with ten mules. The mules always knew exactly what time it was, and at noon they stopped dead, refusing to work until they were turned loose and fed. At six o'clock they would stop, bray, and head for home. Once Walker tried to stick it out, and soon found himself clinging to the wreckage of the plow, with ten mules cantering merrily to the barn. After that, he let them have their way.

Plutarch wrote of the oxen of Susa, who could count to a hundred. The oxen spent their lives carrying water to the royal gardens, and every ox carried one hundred buckets a day. More could not be extracted from them, even by force.

Birds That Bark, and Other Noises

Strange noises near water can often be attributed to fish, which have a surprising array of vocal talents. Unfortunately, field guides rarely include fish calls. Actually, there are very few fish which do not make noises. Most of them can't be heard by humans, although they do fall within the range of our hearing, because our ears are not adapted to hearing in water. Only when a fish is really hollering can we pick it up.

Ocean fish are noisier than freshwater fish. Fish in the tropics have a larger vocabulary than northern fish. And fishes' voices get deeper with age, except for trout, which remain sopranos all their lives.

A loud slurping noise coming from the ocean may be that of a sunfish dining on jellyfish.

The gurnard is a fish which grunts when a thunderstorm is brewing. It is more reliable than human meteorologists. When fishermen in the Mediterranean hear it grunting, they head straight for home.

The pistol shrimp makes a noise so loud it can shatter glass.

Parrotfish graze in herds with their backs sticking out of the water. They chew coral so loudly that you can hear them if you are nearby. They also make themselves nightgowns out of mucus to sleep in every night.

With few exceptions, birds do not sing while on the ground. They sing during flight, or while perched above the ground.

The white-bellied go-away bird distinctly screeches "Go away" upon sighting a human being.

The red-wattled plover of the Middle East shrieks loudly, "Did ya do it?"

Just before it rains, the red-chested cuckoo calls, "It will rain."

Bitterns of Europe boom like foghorns or moo like cows.

The small European duck called the garganey gives a curious "crackling" call reported as sounding "like a single match being rattled in a matchbox."

The spotted bowerbird makes a sound exactly like the crackling of underbrush in a forest fire. It can also imitate an eagle so well as to make chickens run for cover.

L. H. Smith wrote a book in 1968 that told of a lyrebird that lived over nineteen years in the area around an Australian farm. Over the years, the bird learned to imitate: horses neighing, pigs squealing, dogs howling, most bird songs, music from violin, piano, or cornet, the rattling of chains, sawing noises, and human remarks such as "Look out, Jack" and "Gee up, Bess."

Two crested larks in Bavaria learned to imitate a shepherd's whistled commands to his dog: "Run away! Fast! Halt! Come here!"—all of which the dog obeyed.

The Goliath heron lives near the Red Sea and the Persian Gulf. It bays like a hound.

The cagora, a bird found only in New Caledonia, can't fly and barks like a dog.

Everglades kites utter sheeplike bleats while turning somersaults in midair.

The capercaillie is a large turkeylike fowl of Europe. When the males are displaying, they begin with a rattling cry, quickly followed by the pop and gurgle of a bottle being opened and poured, and their performance ends with loud crashing noises. They are so enraptured with their performance that they are oblivious, and can be approached and caught by hand.

The only noise produced by the olivaceous cormorant is a piglike grunt.

David McKelvey had an Indian shama thrush, one of the birds reputed to be the world's best mimics. Named Sam, this thrush could imitate thirty-three species of birds, two mammals, and two amphibians. One of his favorite tricks was to wait in a tree until a jungle fowl happened by, scratching for worms. If the fowl found a worm, Sam would screech like a chicken hawk, sending the fowl scurrying. Then Sam would fly down and eat the worm with satisfaction.

George M. Sutton of the University of Oklahoma watched with interest on May 20, 1951, in Tikal, Guatemala, as a laughing falcon began its irrepressible performance. It was soon joined by a blackbird (*Dives dives*), which began dancing in perfect unison to the laughter, leaping nearly a foot in the air to each syllable, and pausing when the laughing falcon paused. The duet ended when the falcon flew off.

The spotted honeyguide, which is related to the bird that leads humans to beehives, mews like a small kitten.

The European storm petrel purrs and hiccups.

Barnacle geese were once thought to be born inside barnacles. Their call sounds like the yapping of a small terrier.

The bolboceras beetle of Australia sounds like a whining puppy.

The dusky gopher frog of the American Gulf Coast has a voice that sounds like a snore or an outboard motor.

The wood frog, which wears a robber's mask, quacks like a duck.

Eastern narrow-mouthed toads bleat like lambs.

The Mexican tree frog sounds like a car having trouble starting.

Carpenter frogs get their name from their song, which sounds like two workmen hitting a nail in succession. A chorus of these tiny American frogs sounds like a busy construction project.

The Mexican burrowing toad calls "Whoa" like a farmer halting his mule.

Alligator males bellow for their beloveds with a roar that can be heard for a mile, while emitting vapory jets from their chins.

A new electric locomotive near Lake Winnipeg made the same whistle as wapiti during breeding season, and all the male wapiti in the area charged the train until somebody changed the whistle.

Barking deer, that live in Java, Sumatra, and Borneo, bark like small dogs and make strange clapping noises when alarmed.

Mice sing. Authorities have recorded mice twittering, warbling, whistling, and chirping like birds. In the 1940s the American public was treated by a concert on the radio, performed by a mouse.

The Weddell seal makes a whistle that sounds like falling bombs.

Feasts for Beasts

Flies that ate toads were observed in August 1982 near Portal, Arizona. This was the first record of the horsefly genus *Tabanus* eating a vertebrate. The horsefly larvae were trapping spadefoot toads, stinging them, and sucking out their blood and body fluids.

Several giant South American toads were sent to a university and stored with young, foot-long alligators. One day an alligator was missing, and, sure enough, an X-ray revealed it, whole, curled up, in the belly of a toad.

Praying mantids have been known to capture and eat hummingbirds and field mice.

C. W. Monckton, stranded on the desolate Trobriand Islands, noticed that the only other inhabitants, gangs of rats, were lining up on the shore and dangling their tails in the water. They would wait until a crab bit, and then haul it out and gobble it up.

The web-throwing spider of South Africa disguises itself as a tree bud by day. At night, it weaves a rubbery web the size of a postage stamp between its legs and waits for prey to blunder by. When it spots a likely victim, it flings out the web so that it expands to six times its original size and nets the morsel, like a gladiator in ancient Rome.

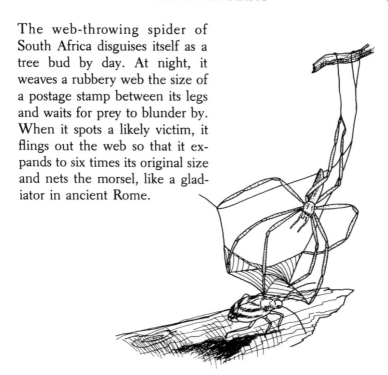

Blue tits, a kind of bird, have been stealing milk from English doorways for decades. They lift the bottles, pierce, drill, or twist them open, or simply fling them into the air to get at the milk.

When earthworms are plentiful, moles bite their heads off and store them underground. If they forget where they put them, the worms will grow new heads and worm away.

Harvester crabs (*Thephusa*) live in the waters of India. They cut grass with their claws, tie it into sheaves, and carry it to their burrows, to be eaten when it ripens into hay.

In the English Channel there dwells a small worm that lives on a garden within itself. The *Convoluta* eats algae when young, until it turns emerald green as the algae plants begin to grow inside its transparent body. It substitutes sunbathing for eating, since the plants provide all the nutrients it needs. Eventually, its mouth and digestive system degenerate from lack of use.

Grebes and dabchicks swallow their own feathers, apparently to aid their digestion.

Octopi sometimes prefer to eat their own kind rather than any fish they are offered.

Human beings and camels are the only mammals that do not eat their placentas.

Baby robins eat fourteen feet of earthworms daily.

The young of the polyphemous moth, which feed on broad-leaved trees, increase their body weight 80,000 times in just two days.

Shrews have such a high metabolism that they can starve to death two or three hours after a meal.

Baby sperm whales gain two hundred pounds a day. Baby blue whales drink more than a ton of milk a day.

When Mount Etna erupted in 126 B.C., the Mediterranean Sea boiled violently, and thousands of perfectly cooked fish washed onto the beaches of the island of Lipari. Some people ate so many fish that they died.

The *New York Post* wire service of February 6, 1985, reported that a Yalta film production of "Bambi" had come to a halt. Three of the four fawn stars had disappeared, and a police investigation discovered that they ended up as the main course at a birthday party.

The pre-Inca natives of the New World had very few domesticated animals—no cattle, sheep, pigs, or goats. Instead they raised guinea pigs for their meat.

The honey possum sucks honey from blossoms.

The hyrax looks like a rabbit but is the nearest living relative of the elephant. One species lives on Mount Kenya and comes out at night to feed on violets.

A forest ranger once left his car window open and found on his return that a porcupine had eaten the steering wheel, leaving only the spokes. Porcupines crave salt, and it seems the wheel had been sweated on to perfection.

A bear once dug through the supplies of some campers in Canada. He found a twenty-pound sack of dried apple chips and devoured them. Later, the bear went to a nearby stream and drank a gallon or two of water. The apple chips swelled so in the poor bear's stomach that he was split from end to end when the campers found him.

Galapagos tortoises eat anything that is red. So zookeepers put their medicine inside tomatoes.

The cigarette beetle lives on a diet of tobacco, chili peppers, mustard, cloves, and anything else that's good and hot.

Man's Best Friends

Sir Henry Wyat, a noble at the court of Richard III (1452–1485) was sent to the Tower of London for political crimes and left to starve. Wyat's pet cat crawled down the chimney every day and brought him a fresh-killed pigeon, keeping him alive for months. King Richard, hearing of the miracle, ordered Wyat released.

John Craig, penniless, friendless, and fleeing a death sentence in Vienna, was befriended by a stray dog that brought him a wallet containing enough money for him to escape home to Scotland.

Rin-Tin-Tin, the world's most popular animal star of his day, was discovered as a shell-shocked puppy cringing in a German trench in World War I by an American serviceman. The GI, Lieutenant Lee Duncan, brought him back to the States and trained him for a film career. The dog provided Warner Brothers Studio with its main source of income for several years.

Ludwig Dobermann was a tax collector in Apolda, Thuringia (Germany), in the 1880s. He was aware of his unpopularity, and so developed a fierce breed of dog to help him collect the taxes. That breed was named Doberman in his honor.

The Chinese train lions to hunt for them. The cats bring down wild bulls and bears, and then wait for the humans to arrive.

The renowned horse trainer Henry Blake described how a poacher was stopped by a police officer, who accused him of using his dog to catch rabbits. The poacher denied this, and took the officer to a field full of rabbits. Then the poacher said, "Go on, boy, catch one," and the dog stood and looked at him with a puzzled expression. After a few minutes of this, the officer gave up and went away disgusted. Then the poacher said to his dog, "Get to heel," and the dog shot out and caught a rabbit.

In Tanganyika, John T. Williamson rested in the shade nearby as a mongrel he had adopted dug the soft earth. The dog uncovered a rock that Williamson saw was a diamond, and the discovery led to his becoming one of the richest men on earth.

A miner and his mule were kicking each other in Idaho when the mule knocked a chunk of rock loose above the miner's head. He picked up the rock to throw at the mule, noticed it was unusually heavy, and discovered the Bunker Hill silver mine.

A farmer asked E. J. Hulbert to help find his lost hog. The hog was found in an old copper mine, which eventually yielded half a million dollars' worth of copper.

An ostrich was found with diamonds in its gizzard in Southwest

Africa, now Namibia. It started a diamond rush in the area, but no more diamonds were found. Ostriches, like lots of birds, swallow stones to aid their digestion.

Ostriches have been used to herd sheep in South Africa. The birds take the sheep out in the morning and bring them back at night. If a sheep dies during the day, the ostriches keep pecking at it; so if they're late, the farmers know a sheep has died.

Baboons have been used with great success as goatherds on the Otjiruse farm in Southwest Africa, in the late 1950s and early 1960s. Dr. Walter Hoesch, the internationally known German zoologist, did a thorough study of a baboon named Ahla that worked for the Aston family on that farm. Ahla was raised from the age of two in the company of goats and fed goats' milk. She was never trained, but accompanied the goats all during the day, rounded up strays, reunited kids and ewes, and knew all eighty goats by sight. The only thing Mrs. Aston had to teach Ahla was not to carry the young kids up trees under her arm for fun. Otherwise she behaved in an exemplary fashion and enjoyed riding on the backs of the big goats.

A rhesus monkey named Johnny drives a tractor in Australia. Johnny opens and closes gates, picks burrs from the sheeps' wool at shearing time, and starts and drives the tractor on command from his master. At lunch time the monkey and the man sit down together and eat and when it is over the monkey tidies up.

James Wide was a signalman on the Port Elizabeth line near Uitenhage, South Africa, in the late 1800s. He lost both legs in a railway accident. From then on, his pet chacma baboon, Jack, kept house, pumped water from the well, and cared for the garden. In the mornings Jack would lock up the shack and push Wide to work in a little trolley. Jack operated the levers that set signals, and he worked so well the railroad company put him on the payroll. The baboon earned 20 cents a day and half a bottle of beer on Saturdays. After nine accident-free years on the job, Jack died in 1890.

Cats have been on the payroll of the British Post Office since the mid-1800s. In 1868, the Secretary hired three female cats at four pence a week each to keep down the rodent population. They proved such a success that more mousers were hired. In 1953, the

Assistant Postmaster General assured the House of Commons that his female cats got "very adequate" maternity benefits and wages equal to the tomcats'. As of 1983, a cat at London's Nine Elms office was getting 1.8 pounds sterling a week.

Gérard de Nerval (1808–1855) was a French poet who strolled daily in the parks of Paris with a live lobster on a leash. When asked why, he said, "Because he knows the secrets of the deep."

Hatteras Jack was a white porpoise who guided ships through Hatteras Inlet off North Carolina from 1790 to 1810, never losing a ship. He would swim around each ship to gauge its size and draw, wait until the tide had reached the proper level, then lead the vessel safely past the treacherous shoals.

The schooner *Brindle* was going through a perilous pass off New Zealand in 1871 when a porpoise started leaping around in front of the ship as if it wanted to lead the way. The ship followed and the porpoise led them safely through. The porpoise was named Pelorus Jack and after that it met and guided every ship that came through. All but one. In 1903, a drunk on the *Penguin* shot at Jack. He disappeared for two weeks and returned to guide every ship but the *Penguin*. In 1909, the *Penguin*, long thought cursed, was wrecked in Pelorus Pass with great loss of life. Jack disappeared in November 1916.

Dolphins and porpoises have often been reported holding drowning people up in the sea or taking them to safety. Yvonne Vladislavich of South Africa was thrown into the Indian Ocean when her yacht exploded in June 1971. Three dolphins approached her and one supported her body while the others patrolled for sharks. They took her to a marker on which she was able to climb. After her rescue it was determined the dolphins had carried her 200 miles to safety.

Candelaria Villanueva was thrown into the sea when the passenger ship she was sailing on sank six hundred miles off the Philippines. She was kept afloat and survived thanks to a sea turtle, which supported her for two days, until she was rescued.

Evelyn Waugh, the writer, once tried to drown himself but failed because a crowd of jellyfish held him afloat.

The Reverend O. F. Roberston of Hartsville, Tennessee, was going blind. The family cow noticed the difficulty with which Robertson got around the farm, and became his self-appointed guide.

A French soldier was wounded in one of Napoleon's battles and was lying in the field. His horse, who had been left behind because it was lame, broke loose and rescued the soldier, who barely had strength enough to climb on his back. He was brought back to the regiment unconscious, lying across his horse with no saddle, bridle, or halter.

Plutarch wrote of Alexander the Great's attack on King Porus of India. The king was mounted on a fine war-elephant who defended him with courage during the battle. When the elephant realized that the king had been wounded with many arrows, it knelt down, and drew out the missiles with its trunk. Porus survived and was taken prisoner.

A woman known only as Old Aunt Tess lived in Hermitage, Tennessee, with her canary, Bibs. One rainy night she fell and cut her head severely, and Bibs flew down the road for help. Old Aunt Tess' niece and husband were sitting by the fire when they heard a tapping at the window. At first they thought it was a branch, but then they heard an almost human cry. The niece ran to the window, drew the curtains, and Bibs dropped dead before her. They drove to Old Aunt Tess' and found her in a pool of blood, but they saved her thanks to poor Bibs.

A boy named Hugh Perkins of Summersville, West Virginia, was laid up in the hospital in 1939. His pet homing pigeon, Billy, travelled a hundred and five miles in ten days and located the correct window ledge of the hospital in Philippi where his owner was. Proof that it was Billy and not some friendly wild pigeon came with the identifying band on his leg.

Beastly Battles

An incident known as the Great Bengal Frog War took place in Malaysia on November 8, 1970. It started as a squabble among about 50 frogs but within hours thousands of frogs had joined the fray and by the end of the week the ground was littered with dead frogs. Biologists said it was actually a vast orgy but could not explain why so many had clawed each other to death.

The Grasshopper Battle was a short war between the Delaware and Shawnee Indians in 1872, which started as a squabble between two children over who owned a pet grasshopper. The Shawnees lost the war and, I assume, the grasshopper, and moved out of the Pennsylvania area where the two tribes had long lived in harmony.

The War of the Stray Dog took place in 1925 when a Greek soldier chased his dog, which had scuttled across the border into Macedonia. A Bulgarian sentry shot him, and Greece invaded Macedonia in revenge. Over fifty men were killed.

One of the many hero dogs of World War II was a German shepherd named Caesar, who served with the Marines in Bougainville, in the Pacific. The Marines were soon cut off from communications, and Caesar carried all their messages through sniper fire. One day, the dog woke his handler just in time for him to hear a grenade pin being pulled nearby. The live grenade bounced into the foxhole, and the Marine, taking a risk, threw it back. It killed eight Japanese.

Dogs in medieval times wore armor to go into battle. King Cambyses of Persia used bands of big shaggy dogs, attacking in formation, to conquer Egypt in 525 B.C. Roman legions, Attila the Hun, Japanese samurai, Spanish *conquistadores*, and American Revolutionary War soldiers all used dogs in battle. The Earl of Essex under Queen Elizabeth I took 800 bloodhounds to suppress the Irish revolt.

Kissingen, Germany, successfully repelled attackers in 1643 by hurling beehives at them.

It is hard to imagine the lowly garden slug as being a useful creature in wartime, but that is what he is. Slugs can detect poison gas in incredibly tiny amounts—one part gas to twelve million parts air—and stop breathing until the gas is gone. Dr. Paul Bartsch of the Smithsonian Institution made this interesting discovery. Slugs will warn people of the presence of gas long before it can harm them, unlike canaries, which drop dead just before a man would.

It sounds like a Hollywood movie, but a pigeon saved the lives of one thousand British infantrymen. During World II, in October 1943, the British 56th Infantry was fighting to take the village of

Colvi Vecchia, Italy, but was stopped by the Germans. The British radioed for air support to pulverize the village. In the confusion, one thousand troops swept into the village only to realize they were about to be killed by their own bombers. The radio had been smashed in the fighting. Their only hope was a single American homing pigeon named GI Joe. GI Joe was sent with the message, which he carried through gunfire twenty miles in twenty minutes, and he reached the airfield just before the bombers were to take off. The pigeon was awarded the Dickin Medal for Gallantry, the first non-British animal to be so honored.

Fighting and
Biting

In the British Museum is an exhibit of the side of a ship with the sword of a swordfish penetrating twenty-two inches into it. Swordfish have been known to attack and sink small boats.

A rattlesnake once sank its fangs into the tire of a car. The compressed air blew the snake to bits.

There are no snakes in Ireland or Hawaii. Every snake in Tasmania is poisonous.

A terrified mother in the United Arab Emirates rushed her one-year-old baby to the hospital when she found it had caught a snake, bit it in half, and was playing with the pieces. Doctors found the tot in perfect health.

An attacking shark will go limp and quiet if flipped on its back.

When two tree-shrews fight, the loser can drive off the winner by flipping on his back and squeaking shrilly. Tape recordings of these "I give up" squeaks send other tree-shrews into convulsions.

The noise of fighter jets can kill mink.

The ant and the assassin bug are two creatures that can kill and eat each other. But the assassin bug has the edge in what zoologists call "the kiss of death." The bug exudes a sweet liquid from glands in its abdomen, offers it to the ant, who devours it greedily, only to be intoxicated and poisoned by the fluid. Calmly and deliberately, the assassin bug grinds through the ant's armor with its razor-sharp nose, liquifies the ant's innards, and devours him.

"The attack, when it came, was sudden and unprovoked," wrote Scott Wiedensaul, of an outing on the Appalachian Trail. "I was pummeled around the head and smacked repeatedly in the face. My ears were soundly boxed." Wiedensaul's companion was unsympathetic. "That's funny," she said. "That butterfly won't leave you alone."

A friend of naturalist Jean Craighead George live-trapped and banded a pair of robins on his Michigan farm. The birds were so traumatized by the event, however, that afterwards they would dive-bomb and hit him with their wings. Changing his clothes and the interval of migration did nothing to dampen their fury. Interestingly, when he drove a tractor, the robins did not recognize him until he got off.

Lemmings, despite their tiny size, are ferocious fighters. A two-ounce lemming will not hesitate to attack a thousand-pound polar bear. Scandinavians say of a valiant man that he is "as brave as a lemming."

Scary Monsters

The most detailed report of man's encounter with a sea serpent was written by Charles Seabury, captain of the whaling ship *Monongahela*. On January 13, 1852, they were whaling in one of the emptiest ocean stretches of the world, in the South Pacific about one thousand miles east of the Marquesas, and three thousand miles north of Pitcairn Island. They came upon a huge sea monster, and a ferocious day-long fight ensued. Early the next morning the creature was killed. It measured 103 feet 7 inches in length, and 49 feet 4 inches around the largest part of the body. It was a male, colored black, brown, yellow, and white. It had ninety-four teeth and four swimming paws, and the end of its tongue was shaped like the head of a heart. The head, heart, bones, and skin were preserved in salt, and the oil, which was "as clear as water," was barrelled. Soon after, the brig *Gipsy* took Captain Seabury's amazing report aboard, along with several barrels of the unique oil. Tragically, the *Monongahela* was lost with all hands later that year, but houses in her home port of Gloucester, Massachusetts, were lighted with sea serpent oil for as long as it lasted.

Giant squids have tentacles as long as telephone poles and eyes the size of basketballs. They are actually rather shy, and avoid sperm whales, with which they have titanic battles.

Pliny wrote of a land serpent 120 feet in length that attacked the Romans besieging Carthage. It could not be driven off, and had to be crushed with huge stones lifted by military engines.

An enormous blob of flesh washed ashore at St. Augustine, Florida, one hundred years ago, and was christened the Florida Monster. It had lost its head and only stumps remained of what presumably had been legs. Some thought it was a dead elephant. Among the first to examine it was Professor A. E. Verrill, an eminent giant squid expert. He thought it was a giant octopus, but hesitated to say so, since it was so gigantic. For two months all six tons of it lay on the beach putrefying. It got so tough an axe couldn't dent it. Microscope slides had been taken, and it has recently been determined to have been a giant octopus, with tentacles about as long as a football field.

Dr. Anton Brun, on board the *Galathea* in the Atlantic, brought up an eel larva six feet long. Since the larva of a freshwater eel is only three inches long, these larvae could be expected to grow to between forty-eight and one hundred feet in length.

The shipwrecked crew of the merchant vessel *Britannia* was forced to deal with dreadful peril in the South Atlantic. During the night, "something" crawled among the men on their makeshift raft and carried one kicking and screaming away. Later, it attacked Lieutenant R. E. G. Cox, who desperately fought it off, and the monster retreated to the depths. After they were rescued, doctors looked at Cox's wounds and concluded that he had been attacked by a twenty-three-foot-long giant squid. The report was made March 25, 1941.

The octopus can squeeze through amazingly tiny openings; climb, jump, and fight on dry land; and give a venomous bite. The tiny blue-ringed octopus, no bigger than a silver dollar, can kill a man with its bite.

Carolus Linnaeus, the Swedish genius who devised the naming

system of living things, was a fervent believer in sea monsters, citing innumerable reports of fishermen.

A book called *Items of Interest Taken from a Sicilian Trip*, published in 1742, described a troublesome multi-colored sea monster off the coast of North Africa that repeatedly tore the fishermen's nets. The entire adult population of several villages worked together to make an especially strong net to catch the beast. Despite their efforts, the net was shredded and the sea monster got away.

In February 1962, Forrest Adrian was using a television camera to check on an underwater oil rig off Santa Barbara, California. He was startled enough to yell when a creature like a giant snake appeared on the screen. The whole crew watched the monster, which was between ten and fifteen feet in length, snakelike, with knobby ridges running around the spiral of its body. It swam by rolling around and around. It was apparently attracted by the lights at one hundred and seventy-nine feet. The Shell Oil crew named it Marvin, "friend of the sea."

Oarfish, which live thousands of feet under the sea, have been captured occasionally when they are in distress. There is one in the San Diego Museum which is twenty-two feet long and weighs six hundred pounds. They are snaky-looking with two spikes on their head and a long ribbonlike fin down the back.

Giant groupers can grow to fantastic size, and the Australian *Sydney Herald* has reported over the years that deep-sea divers have been swallowed whole by groupers, metal helmet, rubber suit, lead shoes and all. Diver J. T. L. Powers rescued his partner by punching a grouper in the eye, so it spit him out.

A mako shark was captured off the Bahamas with a 120-pound swordfish intact in its belly. That means the 730-pound shark swallowed it in one bite.

One of the most terrifying fish is also one of the smallest. The candiru, which infests the rivers of South America, can swim up a stream of urine and into a man's penis, then stick its spines out into the flesh so that it cannot be removed except by surgery. If the fish reaches the bladder, it can kill. South Americans fear this tiny fish much more than they do the piranha, which owes its reputation more to Hollywood than to fact.

The scientist Stewart Springer was bitten by a shark—an embryo sand tiger shark still in its mother.

The huge *Mola mola* can grow to ten feet or more in diameter and weigh over two thousand pounds. The spinal cord is only one inch long. The flesh is rubbery and natives make bouncing balls of it. The mola is startlingly phosphorescent and is sometimes called a "moonfish," for its resemblance to an underwater moon. Fortunately, they have never been known to attack people.

Divers should be wary of the abalone, which can clamp down on their fingers and drown them.

The giant clam *Tridacna*, falsely called a man-eater, can be four feet across and weigh over five hundred pounds. Living giant clams have mantles of brilliant blue-green, violet, and yellow. These huge mollusks sometimes make pearls of a dull finish. The largest pearl is nine and a half inches long, five and a half inches in diameter, and is known as the Pearl of Allah, as it is said to bear an image of Mohammed. This type of clam, which produced the sacred pearl, ironically, is responsible for the only known death of a man. On May 7, 1934, a William Dowell Cobb witnessed the death by clam of a Philippine native.

Crocodiles are intimidated by tall creatures. So if you are charged by one, stand up, raise your hands, and try to look tall and intimidating.

Four-foot worms three-quarters of an inch in diameter now live in southeastern Australia. The gurgling, sucking noises they make are clearly audible above ground. The giant worm eggs are the size of large olives.

In Zimbabwe a farmer was trying to extricate a spitting cobra from his car engine when the snake spat in his eyes, blinding him. An African woman, nursing a baby, saw this happen and squirted her breast milk in his eyes, thus saving his sight.

If you are walking down a jungle path and meet a tiger, don't panic. The best plan (according to Jim Corbett, who lived among and hunted tigers all his life) is to step aside, stand still, and slowly raise one hand, holding the fingers in the manner of Indian temple idols.

Jim Corbett became famous for despatching man-eating tigers and leopards. One of his most fearsome targets was the Champawat man-eating tiger. One of her victims was a young woman, whose sister witnessed the attack and gave chase, yelling and waving a scythe, until the tiger turned on her. The sister was struck dumb from shock for several years. When Corbett finally killed the cat, the young woman regained her voice on seeing the skin. The tiger had killed 436 people.

Another of Jim Corbett's adventures concerned the man-eating Rudraprayag leopard. One night this leopard selected a victim only after stepping over the bodies of *fifty* sleeping pilgrims, without waking them, killing the woman silently, and carrying her body back over the sleeping people. He then escaped into the night.

There is only one record of a mountain lion attack. In 1924, a mountain lion killed a thirteen-year-old boy in Washington State, and then ate him.

A few years ago, a lion escaped from a circus and panicked the citizens of Rome. A drunk wandered up and patted the huge cat on the head and whispered in his ear. The drunk was not harmed.

The following news article is reproduced in its entirety:

A French tourist was stripped of his clothes Wednesday by a male orangutan, which fled with the garments into a forest sanctuary in Malaysia. The tourist, whose name was not released, was walking in an ape sanctuary with his wife when the fourteen-year-old orangutan called Raja confronted him and stripped him. The stunned Frenchman did not move and the ape did not harm him. It fled with his clothes, underwear and all, into the forest. Other tourists later gave the man clothes. "This unusual incident is a warning to all tourists to wear clothes which cannot be removed easily," a park official said. "I think Raja was curious," he added. "We will track it and see if the animal attempts to wear the Frenchman's clothes."

Deutsche Presse Agentur, Hbg Patriot News
October 1992

Huge black rhinos are the most easily tamed of all big game animals in Africa. Once captured, they will eat from a keeper's hand and come on call to have their ears rubbed.

Tasmanian wolves will kill for blood, leaving the meat for scavengers such as Tasmanian devils.

Perhaps the most dangerous inhabitant of the Far North is also one of the smallest. Female blackflies attack in vicious swarms, tearing out chunks of flesh from their victims. They inject a toxic chemical which keeps the blood flowing and makes the wound itch, burn, swell, and sometimes become infected. Man and beast alike can literally go mad because of these pests.

The most dangerous insect in the world is the common housefly. It can carry thirty diseases including typhoid, cholera, dysentery, bubonic plague, leprosy, cerebro-spinal meningitis, diphtheria, scarlet fever, and polio.

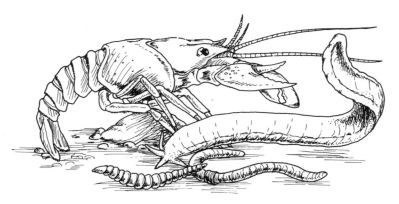

Creatures'
Features

Lobsters are arachnids, like spiders, having eight legs and an exoskeleton. In Colonial times, they were fed only to slaves. The Maine lobster walks forward but flees backwards. It chews sideways and tastes with its feet. Its kidneys are in its forehead. Its teeth are in its stomach. It listens and smells with its legs. It is nearsighted. For no apparent reason, the lobster sometimes dismembers itself. Its blood is blue.

The glutinous hag is one of the most disgusting creatures on earth. It bores into its prey, rasping and boring, until the victim is a mere bag of skin and bones. It is a hermaphroditic fish with one nostril or mouth, degenerate eyes sunk deep under muscle, four hearts, no jaws, stomach, or anus, and so many slime glands that it can convert a bucket of water into a whitish slime in a matter of seconds. If you should get it into your head to grab one, it will tie itself into a knot and roll the knot up and down its body until you let go of it.

The maximum length of a ribbon worm is said to be about 180

feet, and this is no misprint. Ribbon worms can alter their length enormously, contracting from several yards to several inches. The worm *Lineus gesserensis* turns completely inside out on contact with certain irritants in the water. Members of the same class, *Bdellomorpha*, live in the spaces between sand grains, growing to a maximum of two to three millimetres.

Ice worms live inside glaciers and fall to pieces if raised to room temperature. No one knows what they can possibly eat.

Fish of Arctic and Antarctic waters possess a chemical in their bloodstreams, much like antifreeze, which lowers the freezing point. They also share, with shellfish and some insects of these regions, the ability to be partially frozen and still return to life upon thawing.

Penguins have an organ above their eyes that converts sea water to fresh.

Gulls, terns, skuas, and other sea birds that endure the glare of sun on sea have reddish oil in their eyes that acts as built-in sunglasses.

A test made on the visual powers of peregrine falcons in Germany in 1934 showed that the birds could easily see a lure at a distance of 5,400 feet (over a mile) while the same lure could not be seen by a man through binoculars at a shorter distance.

Octopi usually have one small eye to see in well-lit spaces, and one large eye to scan the darkness of the deep.

The squid nervous system and eye have been used for many years in medical research. The squid eye, which is remarkably humanlike, is in some ways better designed. There is no blind spot, the lens moves in and out like a camera lens to focus, and the eye is tilted at an angle so the creature can see a wider angle than people can.

Chimpanzees can distinguish between varying hues of yellow and red two times better than human beings. The only color hedgehogs can see is yellow. The red-backed vole can see only yellow and red, the civet cat red and green. When a frog is frightened it is repelled by the color green and attracted to anything blue, since a leap into water would, of course, be safer than staying on land.

The Cuban boa, which lives in the pitch-black caves of Trinidad, sees bats as low red lights weaving and darting in space like shimmering flames.

Snakes are deaf. If a rattlesnake is prevented from seeing and smelling a mouse, it can still catch it, thanks to two pits that lie between its eyes and nostrils, which enable it to "see" the heat of the mouse's body. If humans had this feature, we would look like giant glowworms to each other.

The family *Phengodidoe*, related to fireflies, produces light in all stages of life, including the egg.

Night herons and barn owls glow in the dark.

There is no blue pigment in birds' feathers, or beetles' or butterflies' wings. Translucent air-filled cells over a black ground disperse the light, creating a blue color. The sky appears blue for the same reason.

A pigeon's feathers are heavier than its bones.

Hummingbirds' hearts beat fourteen hundred times a minute. They are warm-blooded, but revert to their reptilian ancestry when the temperature drops, and become cold-blooded. They can fly upside down, sideways, and rearwards, but they can't walk.

Dragonflies have six legs but cannot walk.

Butterflies taste with their hind feet.

Female crickets taste with their ovipositors.

The catfish can taste and smell with every part of its skin, from whiskers to fins.

According to the late science fact and fiction writer Isaac Asimov, mosquitos have forty-seven teeth.

Crayfishes' teeth are in the stomach. The liver is in the head.

A barnacle's head contains, among other things, its ovaries.

Cockroaches hear with their bellies. They also breathe through their bellies, which is why boric acid (which is used to wash the eyes of newborn babies) is a deadly poison to them. It plugs up their nostrils.

No insects have their ears in their heads.

The opossum shrimp has ears in its tail.

Elephants have acute hearing and can easily detect the footsteps of a mouse. They can also move noiselessly.

Most blue-eyed white cats are deaf.

Horace F. Carpenter, a noted shell authority, states that if cats are allowed to eat the rims of scallops, their ears will fall off. He bases his assertion on an extensive study of cats on the coast of Rhode Island, where an unusual number of earless cats live.

Scallops have between thirty and a hundred blue eyes arrayed around the edges of their lovely shells.

The horned toad, which is actually a lizard, squirts blood from its eyes when alarmed. Raymond Ditmars, a well-known herpetologist, watched a Mexican horned toad squirting a wall four feet away with blood that he said seemed to be coming from its eyelids.

A salamander known as the hellbender breathes through lungs, gills, and also through its skin.

Every part of a newt can regenerate, even the jaws and eyes. In the eighteenth century, the great Italian naturalist Lazzaro Spallanzani cut off the hind leg of a newt 1,374 times, and each time the animal regrew the leg.

A blind chameleon can still camouflage itself to match its surroundings.

Geckos have tiny hooks on their feet which are so effective they can walk across the surface of a mirror.

The basilisk, or "Jesus Christ lizard," can run across the surface of water on its hind legs. The lizards' bodies are light and their feet large, and as long as they do not stop, they will not sink. Witnesses report seeing the lizards dashing over water a quarter of a mile or more in width.

Rain frogs, unlike their water-loving cousins, live in deserts and rarely venture into standing water. If dropped into water, rain frogs easily drown. Their only means of escape is to blow themselves up like tiny pontoon boats and float away.

The American water shrew *Sorex palusfris* can run across the surface of water, using air bubbles trapped in its foot hairs as floats.

Porcupines float.

Porcupines are born encased in a protective sac.

Discus fish nurse their babies. Cells in the skin secrete mucous which the wee ones consume.

Sawfish have long, flat, toothed saws projecting from their faces. Young sawfish are born with a "velvety glove" over their saws to protect their mothers.

The waterbug is a North American insect which has two thousand eyes, and switchblades that it uses to skewer fish, tadpoles, and insects.

The pipefish invented the zipper long before man did. The male pipefish has a long groove in his abdomen, into which the female deposits her fertilized eggs. A thin membrane zips over them, holding them in place for the sixteen days it takes to hatch.

Barnacle glue is twice as tough as epoxy, binds together any materials, and resists all chemicals known to science. At 662 °F (350 °C), it softens only slightly, at −38 ° it does not crack or peel. Three ten-thousandths of an inch of this glue provides a strength of over three tons and holds tighter than scientists have been able to measure. They believe that if a whole barnacle could be pulled from a steel buoy, a layer of steel would come off along with it.

The chiton, a small trident shell, can produce four different minerals without the heat and high pressure needed for the same process deep in the earth. Chiton produce two iron compounds (one of which has never been observed to be made by biological means) that are used to coat its extremely hard teeth.

Bobolinks have tiny particles of iron inside their nasal cavities. R. C. Beason and J. E. Nichols theorized in 1984 that these iron deposits help birds navigate magnetically, like having a built-in compass.

Shrimps and lobsters sense gravity through boxes in the sides of their heads which collect sand. They lose this sand when they molt, so if they are kept in a sandless tank they will flounder around and stand on their heads.

It is believed that the ear originated not as a hearing instrument, but as an organ for maintaining balance.

The jellyfish is not a single animal but a colony of animals. Some tentacles take care of balance, others sting enemies, some catch prey, and others are in charge of breeding.

If a sponge is cut to pieces and squeezed through a screen so that it is just a bunch of loose cells, it will reassemble itself into a completely functioning organism.

Fat-tail sheep, which were bred in far-eastern Asia for the tallow which their fat tails produced, eventually grew tails so fat that carts had to be hitched to the sheep, for the sole purpose of carrying their tails around.

A donkey can't bray if you tie down his tail. A duck can't walk without bobbing its head. A frog uses its eyeballs to swallow, and can't do so without closing them.

All mammals have tongues.

Dogs and cats have a common ancestor.

Zebras have white stripes on black because they are descended from black animals.

The black sheep's reputation comes from its biological rarity; there were never enough of them to market black wool, so it was considered worthless.

Yak milk is pink.

Tapirs have retractable snouts.

The tip of the woodcock's beak is prehensile. It can stick it in the mud and wiggle the end around to catch worms.

Soldiers of the Nasutitermes termites have a squirt-gun nozzle on their heads from which they squirt a gooey mess that entangles their rivals.

Ants have five different noses, for five different purposes.

The autolytus, a worm that lives in the sea, can have as many as eight heads at one time. They reproduce by budding, and each segment has its own head.

The blindworm, also known as the slowworm and the deaf adder, is not blind, nor slow, nor deaf, nor is it even an adder. It is a legless lizard.

The big-eyed wolf spider of Kauai, Hawaii, has no eyes.

The tailless bandicoot, which has a long tail, was named by early naturalists in Australia who found a tailless specimen. They instructed the natives to bring more of the same, and the obliging aborigines chopped off all the tails of the specimens.

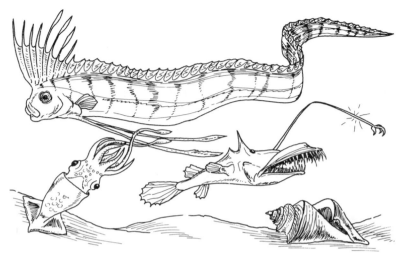

Beautiful Beings

Deep in the sea, where there is no light to see them, live some of the most beautiful creatures on earth. There are forests that eat meat; crinoids, animals that have taken on the appearance of plants. Some are free-moving, some fixed to the bottom with stones. They break into pieces when they are agitated, and their colors are fast only in salt water, fading rapidly on contact with the air, so there can only be a fleeting impression of their beauty.

Sea-dragons are deep-sea fish with luminous spots along their flanks, which make them look very much like ocean liners cruising through the darkness. Their fangs are illuminated from inside their mouths.

Two kinds of fish in Indonesia have luminescent bacteria growing under their eyes, which create beams of light like tiny headlights. They can switch them off and on with a window-shade-like device.

A chaetodon, a kind of fish, is all but invisible in strong light. Its colors grow brighter as light dims. It is brilliantly luminous at night.

The black-hooded squid is adorned with colored lights along its body and spotlights to penetrate the darkness of the deep ocean.

The small squid *Heteroteuthis dispar* ejects a trail of blinding liquid fire to confuse predators.

The freshwater limpet *Latia neritoides* of New Zealand will, if disturbed, fill the gap between foot and mantle with a luminous green mucus which glows visibly in daylight. It will die if kept exposed to light.

Tourists who visit Auckland, New Zealand, are directed to the Waitomo Caves. They contain Glowworm Grotto, which is lit an eerie blue by thousands of gnat larvae who use the lights to trap midges. As the larvae grow, they produce silken threads which hang from the cave ceilings like strings of lights to both attract and snare flying insects.

Fireflies in Thailand and Burma gather by the thousands on particular trees and flash on and off *in unison*.

The railway beetle of Paraguay is three inches long. It blinks red lights at both ends, and green lights in between.

The baya bird of India adds lightning bugs to his nest, illuminating his home.

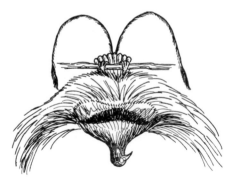

The male Emperor Wilhelm's bird of paradise hangs upside down to display his saffron-yellow and emerald-green breast. He quivers his delicate white wing feathers in an arc around him, suggesting a shimmering fountain. The blue bird of paradise (yes, there is such a bird) also hangs head downwards to display his brilliant blue feathers and arching dark plumes.

The Ruggiana bird of paradise dances along a branch, then spreads his wings above his head to show their rose and pink colors, while pulsing his yellow, green, and black throat to his intended.

The blue-crowned hanging parrot is brilliant green with a bright red throat and rump and blue crown. Despite its spectacular colors, it blends superbly with the tall trees of Borneo and Sumatra. The parrot sleeps hanging upside down like a bat, possibly to make itself less conspicuous.

The words "beautiful" and "bat" don't often appear together, but there are some beautiful bats in the world. The funnel-eared bat looks like a tiny Pekingese with golden fur; the spectacled flying fox has a white face, black eye-rings, and a sleek foxlike head; the yellow-winged bat has large eyes, long silky fur, and brilliant yellow wings; and the Egyptian fruit bat, whose young are born with scrunched-up, humanlike faces, wraps his sweetheart in a protecting wing. These and more are the discoveries of Merlin Tuttle, who is trying to photograph every kind of bat there is and save them from extinction.

Dwarf bushbabies in the wild are often vivid green above and saffron yellow below. These colors fade to a dull gray or brown not only when the animal is stuffed, but also if it is kept alive in a cage. It is thought the colors come from tiny algal spores growing in the fur, which camouflage the animal in the thick forests in which it dwells.

Love Stories

The Great Barrier Reef of Australia is a living colony of animals called coral polyps. It is 1440 miles long and clearly visible from outer space. Every year, all the millions of coral polyps release eggs and sperm *at the same time, on the same night*, in an orgasm of epic proportions.

The heads and brains of palolo worms never participate in their own sex lives. Their rear sections break off and swim to the surface to join other rear ends. The heads remain in the depths, growing new tails.

The female red deer is only in heat for a single day a year.

The female canary may reach adulthood, be provided with a nesting box and a suitable mate, but will not be receptive or lay eggs until she hears the exact melody in the male's song which stimulates her hormones. The more he sings, the faster her eggs develop.

Emperor penguins have sex once a year for two minutes.

The tiny button quail are one of only a handful of birds who have switched sex roles. The brighter-colored females battle each other for the privilege of mating. Once the eggs are laid, the males take over.

A female bird called the red-necked phalarope woos the male, lays the eggs, and deserts him to all the work.

A female egret will only accept a male she considers beautiful. Tall ones with long feathers are the most attractive; shorter males can improve their chances by mixing their courting dance with graceful flights. The smaller the male, the more he has to leap about doing exhaustive acrobatics. In this way he can compensate for his physical shortcomings with charm.

Sanford's golden-crested bowerbird builds a circus ring on the mossy floor of a palm forest. He decorates the edges with the sparkling wings of beetles, the shells of snails, and colorful chunks of resin. Around the treasures he hangs a curtain of bamboo and ferns dangling from the vines above. Every day, the male rearranges his decorations or poses like a weightlifter, hopping about and making chirring noises. If a female is drawn, they will copulate behind the curtain.

To attract females, the satin bowerbird plants two rows of straight twigs in a sort of avenue leading to a "dance floor." He carpets the floor with grass, and collects colorful objects to adorn it. Perhaps to match his blue eyes, he chooses blue flowers, berries, feathers, and bits of blue glass. He then surrounds the dance floor with walls of delicate twigs, painting the inside of the wall with the juice of crushed berries, sometimes using a piece of bark as a paintbrush. He finishes his masterwork with a tasteful arrangement of yellow flowers to set off the blue background.

Bearded tits court during their first spring and become "engaged" (the choice is made by seeing how long the female can endure the male's pecking at her). If they get along well, the male will not stray from the female's side. They bathe, preen, sleep, and look for food together. They caress each other by running their beaks through each other's feathers. Other birds leave the two alone. The following spring, they mate. From then on, the "husband" always spreads out his wings to keep his mate warm at night.

The now extinct huia, a bird of New Zealand, literally could not live without a mate. They lived on insect larvae that bored tunnels deep in trees. The male huia had a short beak which he used to pry bark off trees. The female had a long curved beak she used to extract the larvae, which she shared. If one was killed, the other starved. Maoris wiped out the huia in 1907 by luring them with distress calls.

R. A. Stamm experimented with lovebirds, to see how faithful they were under abnormal conditions. He separated Romeo and Juliet with a glass wall, and gave them both alternative partners. They spent months crouched next to the glass, calling and looking mournfully at each other. When mating season came, they mated with other birds, but returned whenever they could to the glass. When Stamm removed the glass, they instantly abandoned their new mates and were again inseparable. Not all mates were as devoted as Romeo and Juliet, and longer separations tended to make other pairs drift apart. Lovebirds feed their mates, beaks touching. They kiss in greeting, when threatened, before mating, and when making up after a quarrel. Only mates kiss.

The male of some spiders courts the female by waving his conspicuously banded appendages. She is induced to go into a trance-like state during which he safely mates with her.

The male *Nephila* orb-weaving spider weighs a thousand times less than the female. He is so near to nonexistent, he can crawl all over her and leave his sperm in her pocket without ever attracting her attention.

The common male crab spider lassoes his mate, one foot at a time, until all eight legs are safely tied down. Then he spins lines across her abdomen, back, and head before finally mating.

The male *Graphnoid* spider ties down his mate to avoid being killed. This is the common house spider you see hanging in corners. He waits for a female to shed her skin and become helpless, snatches her, wraps her in silk, gets his pedipalpi in her pocket, and escapes. She later awakes like a sleeping beauty, removes her shroud, and walks away.

The beautiful black-and-orange garden spider has invented a long-distance telegraphing system to court the female. He seizes a strand of her web and strums it to get her attention. If in a foul mood, the female communicates her intention to attack by vibrating the web, and the male quickly rappels to safety. If receptive, the female will respond gently, and they communicate until he senses it is safe to approach.

The male tarantula wanders in near-blind state in search of a mate. If he bumps into a female, he beats her with his four front feet. When she rears to retaliate, he clutches her fangs with special claws, drums on her abdomen, and mates.

The male loligo, a kind of squid, mates with a blow to the chin.

Male narwhals may use their single "unicorn" tusk as a lance to duel over females.

Perhaps the most awe-inspiring of all mating rituals takes place between blue whales. They are the largest creatures that have ever existed; they can weigh 400,000 pounds, or twice the weight of *Brachiosaurus*, the heaviest dinosaur. They dive deep into the sea and shoot out of the water, belly to belly. They mate in mid-air.

The male fiddler crab, along with hundreds of his fellows, waves his outsize white claw to attract the female's attention. If a female approaches, he dances, curtsies to her, and dashes into his burrow in hopes she will follow. If she declines, the male comes out and waves frantically at the departing lady.

The female green bonellia, which lives in the sea and looks like a pickle, has a proboscis a yard long with a leaf shape at the end. This is a magic wand. When sexless newborn bonellias are touched by it, they turn into males, make their way to her oviduct, to spend their days fertilizing her eggs as they pass by, assembly-fashion. If a newborn is not touched, it becomes a female with the same magical powers as her mother.

When two snails meet, they mate without having to figure out which sex the other is, since all snails are both. Wooing consists of a long slow dance during which they press together and caress each other with their eyestalks. Then they shoot each other with small harpoons and exchange sperm. Afterward, both wander away to lay eggs.

A small perchlike fish of central Europe lays its eggs and sperm in clams. The clams, in turn, clamp onto passing fish and become worms under the skin. The male fish is not stimulated by the sight of the female; he produces sperm when he sees the clam.

Male anglerfish grab females shortly after they hatch and never let go. The skin of the growing female spreads over the male, her blood vessels connect with his, his mouth disappears, until he becomes a small sex appendage whose only function is to fertilize her eggs.

The male salamander keeps watch for a female taking a stroll, then he dashes in front of her and saunters along, dropping packets of sperm in her path. She either walks over them or picks them up and puts them in her cloaca.

Male garter snakes gently rub their chins along their female's back.

Male Physalaemus frogs of Central America have a dilemma. At mating time, they have to sing lustily to attract a mate. However, if they sing too loud, they attract the Trachops cirrhosus bat, which likes to eat them.

The mating of alligators is a delicate operation. The female takes the initiative by nuzzling the male and climbing all over him. They stroke each other's head, blow bubbles at each other, and cough politely. The act itself entails a lot of maneuvring, until the male is in position at right angles to the female alligator. According to author Diane Ackerman, they "look like mating Swiss Army knives."

The female Photuris firefly answers the signal of the male of her species by blinking her light 2.1 seconds later, and after mating devours him. She knows the signal codes of at least 12 other species of firefly, and answers the males of each with the correct password, luring them all to their doom.

Male bees attract females by taking on the scent of orchids.

The queen bee grows wings on a diet of royal jelly and hums a piping call through the hive to the male drones, whose only function is to mate. The queen flies off with the drones, in pursuit, higher and higher, until the weakest die from exhaustion. The victor mates in a violent act that shatters his wings and tears his legs apart. The queen returns to earth, with a stash of sperm that will last a lifetime (ten to twelve years) of egg-laying.

The swarming of bees has been commented on for centuries but only recently has it been better understood. It was long thought that the queen bee initiated a swarm, but now it appears she is forced out. For several weeks, the queen is fed less and less, until for sixteen days before the exodus she is starved. The worker bees jump on her and shake her, making her nervous. She tries to murder the young queens but is stopped. For five days, she toots in distress. Finally, hundreds of bees cluster on her and force her into the open, and they set off on a search for a new place to live.

A Professor Regan once had a male cricket telephone a female cricket. The female immediately tried to climb into the receiver.

A Dr. Loher demonstrated the true dedication of scientists by first mastering grasshopper language with his tongue, then calling like a female to a male grasshopper. The male jumped toward him, landed on his hand, his arm, and finally in his open mouth!

When a female glowworm is ready to mate, on warm summer evenings, she crawls up a handy grass stem and waves her glowing green abdomen in the air. Males flying low overhead drop like bombs on her, usually hitting with an audible whack. Once mating is accomplished, the lady extinguishes her lamp.

Adactylidium mites mate inside their mother, devour her from inside, and the females are born pregnant. The males are born dead or dying.

Termites use their eyes only once in their entire lives, on the day of their wedding flight.

The female akoushi, a sort of large guinea pig, is only fertile for a few hours so the male has to work fast. First he squeals like a baby akoushi, arousing her maternal instincts so she approaches. Then he trembles violently. Finally he turns his back and pretends to flee by running in place. At this point she usually can't resist him.

Twenty-four rabbits released by a clergyman in Australia in 1859 became twenty-two million rabbits in six years.

Only about five percent of all mammals are monogamous. Fish species are even less likely to stick with a single mate, and in other groups monogamy is all but nonexistent. Birds are the most likely to be faithful, mostly because the young need both parents to feed them.

The two-toed sloth is the only mammal (other than man) that commonly mates face to face. They do so by hanging by their arms from trees.

Making
Themselves
Useful

The Indian monitor lizard is used by burglars in India. The thief ties a rope around the lizard and sends it up a wall. The lizard will find a crack to hide in, wedging itself so securely that it supports the weight of the climbing burglar.

Natives in the South Seas tie a line to a live remora and toss it overboard. Then they only have to wait until the fish attaches itself to a passing turtle or larger fish, then reel them in.

Dead octopi are lowered by fishermen in New Caledonia in places known to be frequented by lobsters. The lobsters spot the octopus, freeze rigid (in terror, they say), and are collected easily by hand.

Deep under the surface of Lake Baikal in Siberia lives a weird fish the locals call *golomianka*. The fish are eight inches long with big popeyes, and they burst when brought to the surface, leaving a vitamin-rich oil slick. The Buryats collect it for lamp oil and medicine. The female fish give birth to two thousand live young at a time.

The candlefish of the Pacific is used literally as a candle by North American Indians. The Indians thread a wick through the fish's body, and when this is lit, the body fat burns steadily. Or the whole fish can be set on fire, to be used as a torch.

In pitch-black caves of South America live crow-size brown birds called oilbirds. They navigate with sonar, like bats, and stuff their chicks with so much palm fruit that they weigh twice as much as their parents do. Native tribesmen have used the oil of these fat chicks to cook with for hundreds of years.

The stomach-oil of the short-tailed shearwater, a sea bird, was used by Tasmanians as a beverage, a vitamin-rich medicine, a lubricant, and as lamp fuel.

Bats are not only tireless insect eaters, they also pollinate a lot of very important plants. Without bats, there would be no avocados, bananas, dates, figs, guavas, breadfruit, peaches, mangoes, carob, cloves, cashews, sisal, kapok, chicle, balsa, or tequila. Trees like the iroko, the durian, and the baobab depend on bats to reproduce. So do organ-pipe cacti and saguaro. Medical science has developed vaccines, birth-control and artificial insemination techniques, navigation aids for the blind, and cryosurgery from bats. And bat guano is an excellent fertilizer.

Thais, or dye shells, are among the most widespread and plentiful of all shells. The *Thais* animal secretes a fluid called purpurin, which can be green, scarlet, or deep purple, and is often used in dye-making.

The sponge has a long and distinguished history. Sponges were first harvested by Phoenicians and Egyptians, and the ancient Greeks used sponges to pad their helmets and leg armor. The men who dove for deep-water sponges became so proficient that diving was introduced into the original Olympic Games. The natural sponge does not burn, so it is in demand by glassmakers to wipe hot glass. Recent research finds some medical benefits as well. The red-beard sponge contains a poison that kills many microbes and viruses, including the fierce staphylococcus that is resistant to penicillin. This sponge has also potential benefits in the treatment of tuberculosis, trench mouth, and bladder disease.

Sharks are immune to cancer, a fact of great interest to researchers. Robert Langer, a biochemist at the Massachusetts Institute of Technology, has isolated the protein that inhibits tumor growth. Powdered shark cartilage in pill form cures cancer in the laboratory. Sharks have no bones, and their cartilage gives off a substance that cuts off the blood supply to tumors. Even newer research shows shark cartilage is very effective against Kaposi's syndrome and other AIDS-related conditions. Potentially, sharks could save more people than they've killed.

Sharkskin is used to make wallets that foil pickpockets. The skin has little teethlike spines which run one way, like fur on a cat's back. If the wallet is slipped into a pocket with the teeth pointing up, it can only be removed with difficulty.

The severe electric shock from electric rays was once used to cure gout. It was discontinued when it was found that most people preferred the gout.

A telegram was sent to Eleanor Roosevelt from the 1939 World's Fair using only the current of electric eels.

Windowpane oysters produce a shell which is used for windows in many parts of the world. They are translucent, not transparent, and ideal to filter out the hot tropical sun. They can also survive hurricanes.

Locals of Norfolk Island, Australia, eat drummer fish, which they call "dreamfish." Eating them gives vivid dreams, hallucinations, and sometimes feelings of paranoia.

Japanese soldiers in World War II made night lights sufficient to read maps by without attracting attention. They ground up crabs to a powder, then added water to make a faint blue light.

The *Nephila* orb-weaving spider spins a web up to eight feet across in the jungles of New Guinea. The Papuans come along, scoop it off, and use it as ready-made fishing nets, waterproof and strong enough to catch a one-pound fish. Native girls in Madagascar collect these spider webs and spin them into textiles. The threads glisten like gold and are lighter and stronger than silk.

Spiders' silk has long been used in the lenses of gun sights, bomb sights, and surveying instruments. It is finer and stronger than anything made by man. One pound of spider web would stretch fifteen thousand miles.

Gall wasps deposit their eggs under the bark of oak trees. The oaks grow a thick lump called an ink ball or oak apple, which contains a dark fluid. The fluid can be used as ink, dye, or to tan leather.

The honey guide is a bird which can find bee's nests but can't break them open. So it calls and flutters around to attract a ratel, or honey badger, who tears open the nest with his strong claws and the two share the spoils. African tribesmen also follow the honey guide, and leave a chunk of wax and honey for the helpful bird.

Pigeons carry microfilm design data from the Lockheed Sunnyvale, California, plant to the test base in the Santa Cruz mountains thirty miles away. It takes half the time it would by car, and is cheaper and safer than a courier service. The fifteen trained birds have never made a mistake, or gotten lost, since January 1982.

Turkey buzzards are used to find gas leaks in southern California. The utility companies add a substance that arouses the buzzards' mating instincts. Excited birds quickly gather around a break in the line, pointing the way for utility repair people.

Defenses and Disguises

The crab *Lybia* of the Indian and Pacific oceans has a soft shell, feeble legs, and is defenseless. So *Lybia* carries a poisonous sea anenome in each claw to sting attackers.

The brittle starfish snaps off all its arms when attacked.

If kangaroos are pursued by dogs, they will hide underwater, catch the dogs with their hands, and drown them.

Baby hoatzin birds hide from predators in waters infested with piranhas. The piranhas don't attack because the birds have a piranha-repellent.

The sea cucumber will, if attacked, spray its attacker with its internal organs. The predator may become entangled and poisoned in the mess, while the sea cucumber rests on the sea floor. Resembling a deflated balloon, it quietly begins to regrow its innards, a process that may take two years.

The larvae of the *Cassida* beetle strike its enemies with a bag of its own feces.

If a krill, a kind of shrimp, is attacked, it will literally jump out of its own shell. The predator is as likely to chase the shell as the shrimp, so the krill has a chance to escape.

A fish called the sea hedgehog is covered, like its namesake, with sharp quills. If a shark is foolish enough to swallow one, the sea hedgehog inflates itself, irritates or punctures the shark's belly with its spines, makes its escape, and calmly swims away.

The Nassau grouper, a Caribbean fish, can change the pattern of its scales eight times in a few minutes to blend in with the colorful coral.

The spider *Cyclosa mulmeinensis* of southeast Asia makes dummies of itself out of bits of web and leftover insect, and strews them about its web. Birds that eat spiders are as likely to grab an imitation as the real thing.

The puss-moth caterpillar can put on a new "face" by pulling down a fold of skin. Like a Halloween mask, it is bright red with a fierce mouth and big scary eyes. At the same time, what looks like a serpent's tongue pokes out from its hindquarters, presumably sending potential predators scattering.

The insect known as the walking leaf lives in Sri Lanka. Its mimicry of a leaf is perfect in every detail; it is shaped and colored like one, is streaked with veins, and even has nibbled yellow edges as if some other bug was eating it. When the wind blows, the walking leaf wiggles gently in unison with the real leaves.

The Kallima butterfly of India looks exactly like a dead leaf, down to rib line and veins. It nests exclusively on shrubs that shed dead leaves in the growing season.

The moth *Stenoma algidella* gets my vote for most effective disguise. It looks exactly like a bird dropping.

Peppered moths of England have survived because their normally white wings have darkened in recent years, allowing them to blend in with the polluted tree trunks on which they live. This is the most spectacular and best-documented case of adaptive evolution, the core of Darwin's theory.

An African millipede, **Aphloria corrugata,** drenches attackers in deadly clouds of hydrogen cyanide. The poisonous gas is fired through vents like portholes along the bug's flanks, from both sides at once if needed.

The bombardier beetle shoots jets of boiling-hot quinine at its attackers.

The spray of a skunk glows with phosphorescent light.

The moonrat defends itself by exuding the odor of onions.

When common shrews are frightened, one baby grabs the base of its mother's tail with its teeth. Another grabs the first baby's tail and so on until they can escape linked together. If the mother jumps over an obstacle, the babies jump with her, and they start and stop as one.

Brush rabbits and desert cottontails both climb trees to escape being eaten.

The white-sided jackrabbit does not simply run away. When a predator comes close it explodes from hiding, then quickly flashes light and dark by shifting the white of its belly fur up its flanks and pulling the black fur of its sides to its belly, all the while running and swerving at full tilt. The performance ends with a disappearing act. The jackrabbit comes to an abrupt halt, crouches down, and flattens its ears. The pursuer's eye continues to track where it thinks the jackrabbit has gone, and so loses its meal.

Wee Beasties

When English biologist J. B. S. Haldane was asked what organic evolution had revealed about God's design, he said, "An inordinate fondness for beetles."

According to George Stimson, who writes books to, as he says, "satisfy his curiosity," "So far as science has been able to discover, there are no two objects in the world exactly alike, no matter whether they are natural or artificial. No two leaves or snowflakes, no two objects manufactured by man, are exactly alike. Scientists believe that even each infinitesimal atom composing the elements differs from all the rest."

Convoluta paradoxa is a worm which is a plant, an animal, a male, a female, and so small that you can fit 436,000 of them in a cubic inch.

The smallest insects are called fairy-flies and live within the eggs of other insects.

A wingless fly only half an inch long is the largest animal that lives in Antarctica year round.

Thirty thousand army ants went marching off in the American Museum of Natural History, and have never been found.

Primitive forms of life have been discovered buried inside meteorites. The microscopic organisms are shield-shaped and covered with spines.

Bacteria can survive on the moon. Colonies inadvertently left by *Surveyor III* were found alive three years later. Ten-thousand-year-old bacteria found in Antarctica in 1974 were revived and reproduced.

METRIC CONVERSION CHART

Common Meas.	Multiply by	Approx. Metric
Length/Distance		
inches	25.4	millimetres
inches	2.54	centimetres
feet	30	centimetres
yards	.91	metres
miles	1.6	kilometres
Weight		
ounces	28	grams
pounds	.9	kilograms
ton (short)	1.1	ton

Index